Discovering The A B C'S OF New Orleans

Written & Illustrated By

Tanyell Ellis

THIS BOOK BELONGS TO

_____

_____

_____

A is for Alligator in the swamp.

Cafe du Monde

813 Decatur St

Saturday- Sunday
7:30AM-11PM

B is for bookoo Beignets at Cafe du Monde.

SPICY
Shell
Mudbugs
HOT
Live
BITE

C is for Crawfish Cookout.

PINCH

YUM!

Tails

Season

MILD

PEAL

BOILED

-

D is for dancing
in the streets.

E is for Etoufee with shrimp and okra.

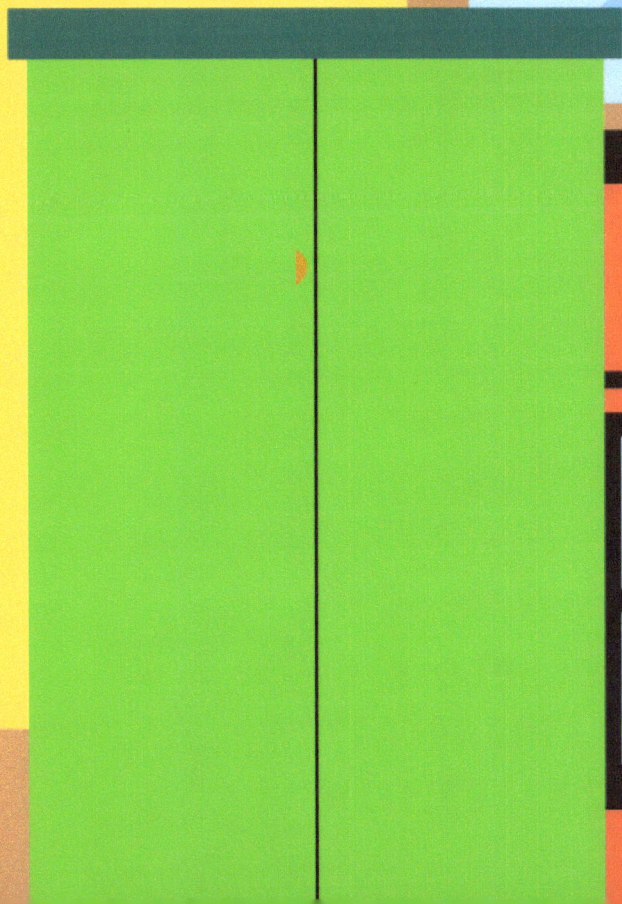

KAYDEN'S
ICE CREAM FESTIVAL

$2 CHOCOLATE
$2 STRAWBERRY
$2 NEAPOLITAN

F is for festival with friends, family, and lots of fun.

Ruby ST

LEE ST

Willow
Ice-Cream CO.

G is for Gumbo
just like grandma
made it.

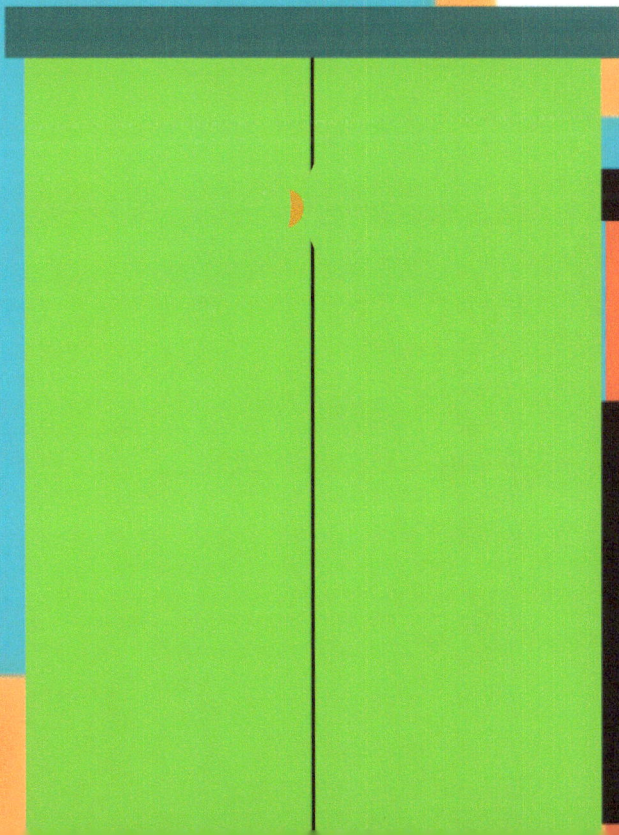

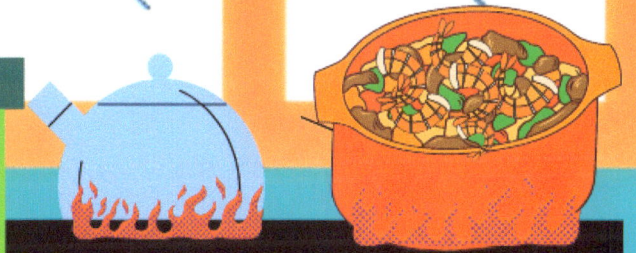

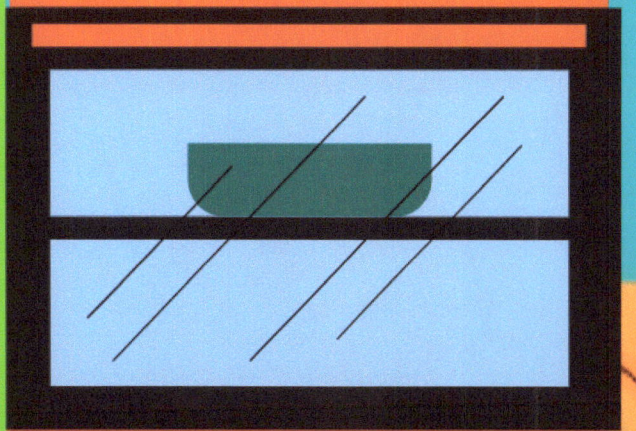

H is for Hurricane so we need to prepare.

I is for Indians making a new suit for carnival.

Ruby Red

J is for jazz at Louis Armstrong Park.

K is for King Cake
with lots of
yummy icing.

L is for Levees protecting our homes.

M is for music all around.

N is for New Orleans, the Big Easy.

Terrell's
Skate Shop

TRINITY-TEMPLE DAY SPA

Come Roll with me!

O is for Oysters off
the grill.

P is for yummy Praline candy with pecans.

KASH
CANDY STORE

Q is for quacking ducks
in the pond at City Park.

QuacK

QuacK

QuacK

R is for Red Beans
on a Monday.

S is for the Second line. We like to step, skip, and hop in the streets.

T is for Trinity seasoning celery, onion, bell-pepper, and Tchoupitoulas street.

TCHOUPITOULAS ST

U is for umbrella
on rainy day or

swinging it around at a secondline on a Sunday.

Krewe of Fun

V is for vanilla stuffed
ice-cream snowball.

Snowballs

Mon- Sat
11am-6pm
Sun
11am-2pm

Flavors

almond	dreamsicle
apple	fruit-punch
bannana	grape
bubblegum	green-apple
cherry	Hawaiian
candy apple	ice-cream

W is for Who-Dat fans all around.

X is for Xavier University.

Y is for Yummy food
in my tummy.

Z is for Zydeco
dancing and fun.

We have learned the exciting Alphabets of New Orleans.

Now it's your time to find exciting new ABC's on your own.